how to have fun making christmas decorations

By Editors of Creative

Illustrated by Nancy Inderieden

7602

DEDICATED TO
TOM, MIKE, KRISTY and TIMMY

WITH A SPECIAL THANKS TO SUE

creative
craft
book

Library of Congress Number: # 73-20197
ISBN: # 0-87191-292-9

Published by Creative Education, Mankato, Minnesota 56001. Distributed by Childrens Press, 1224 West Van Buren Street, Chicago, Illinois 60607

4

ABOUT CHRISTMAS DECORATIONS

Christmas is the happiest and busiest time of the year for children all over the world. Decorating for this merry holiday is a very special time.

In England one of the most important decorations for the children is their Christmas stocking. They hang them by their fireplaces for "Father Christmas" to fill with Christmas treats.

Mistletoe is used for decorating the homes in France. This is a symbol of good luck.

Some homes in Germany have Christmas trees for every member of the family. Each tree is decorated with lights and candy.

Mexican children have piñatas. They are made of papier-mache and filled with gifts and candy. Then the children are blindfolded and by using sticks they try to break the piñata which has been hung up. Then they scramble to get the gifts and candy.

People in Canada and the United States use holly, mistletoe, and Christmas trees to decorate their homes. The cities, towns, and villages sparkle with bright lights and decorations. Many people even decorate their lawns and the outside of their house with decorations, lights, and Christmas trees.

For weeks before Christmas families are busy decorating and making special Christmas cakes, cookies and candy. It is one time of the year when all children can help to decorate.

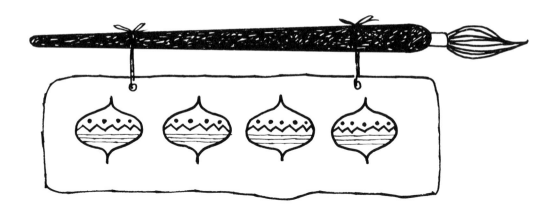

LET'S BEGIN

We will start with some very easy Christmas decorations. You will be able to do these by yourself. They do not use any special materials. You will probably not even have to buy any supplies.

Later, when someone older is able to give you a little help you can make the other decorations.

Always be sure that you have a good work area and time to complete the project. Have fun making your decorations. Add any of your own ideas to them. Make them special. Be pleased with the decorations you make.

Remember, Christmas is a happy time of year. Be happy while making your decorations. Make someone else happy by giving them some of your decorations.

EASY DECORATIONS

The directions for these decorations are not hard to follow. They will not take long to make. But don't hurry too much. Make sure you like your decorations when you are done.

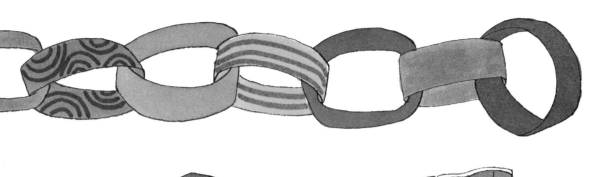

Christmas Tree Strings and Chains

You can make chains and strings to go around your Christmas tree from many different things. Try some of these.

Chains can be made by cutting strips of paper. Each strip should be cut about 1 inch wide and 6 inches long. Put the strings one inside the other and then either glue, tape, or staple them together to make a chain. For paper you can use colored construction paper or gift wrapping paper.

Chains can also be made by taking some aluminum foil and cutting it into strips. Crumple each strip. Squash them together to form the chain. These will really sparkle on your tree.

To make tree strings you will need a needle and thread. Use red or green thread. You can string popcorn or cranberries this way. Watch out for the cranberry ones. They can be messy. When stringing popcorn, put the needle through the soft part of each kernel. Make enough strings so that every other one on your tree is popcorn, and cranberry.

Paper Decorations

By using colored paper, tissue paper and gift wrapping paper you can make all kinds of interesting decorations to hang on your tree, or to decorate your house.

You can cut out Christmas tree shapes and stockings, Santa Clauses, angels, stars, balls, and bells. These same shapes can be used on styrofoam (you can even buy styrofoam balls), or felt too!

Decorate them by coloring, painting, cotton, sequins, glitter, or any special decorations you can find!

Here's an interesting tree ball you can make just by folding a piece of paper. Use the heavy colored paper for this.

Start with a square piece of paper. It should be a heavy colored paper. Mark the corners with a pencil A B C D. Fold the A/C side to the B/D side. Open. Fold the A/B to the C/D. Open. Fold A to D. Open.

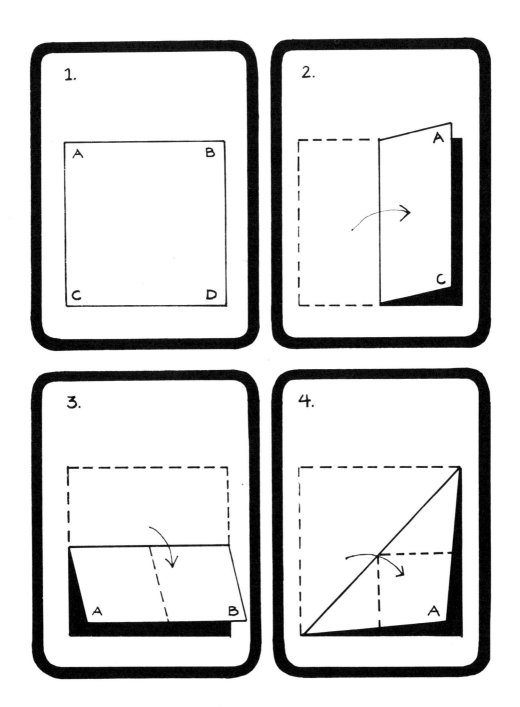

1.

A   B

C   D

2.

A

C

3.

A   B

4.

A

B to C. Open. Now fold the corner with the A to the fold that runs from B to C. Fold both ways—up and down. Open. Do the same with D corner. Now fold the B corner to the line that runs from A to D. And then the C corner.

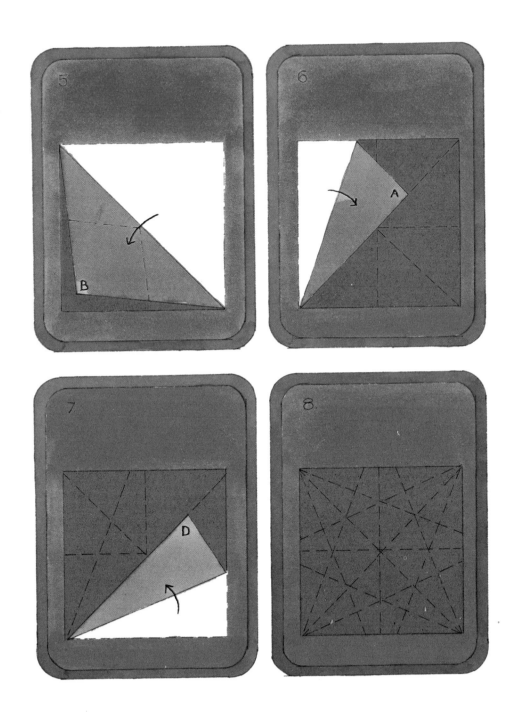

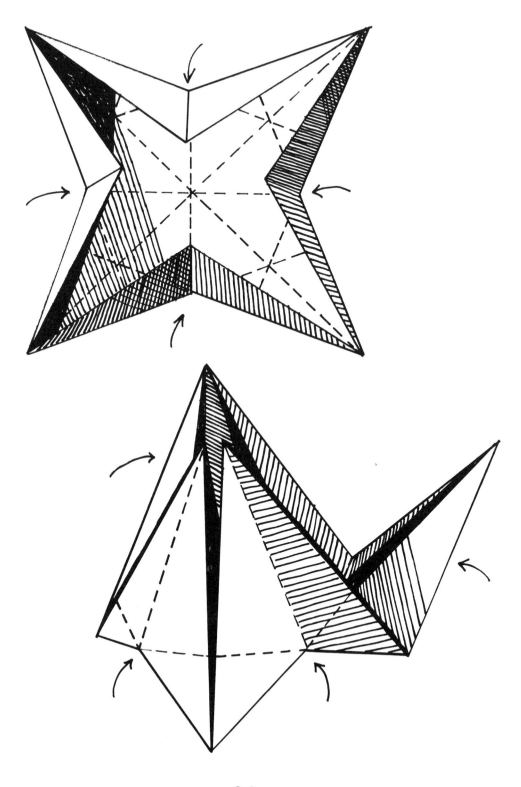

Open it up again. Now begin to make a star by pushing the edges into shape. See diagram. Glue the edges together carefully. Glue the yarn inside the top.

Decorate, and hang.

Other paper balls to hang on your tree can be made by cutting 2 circles from colored paper. Now cut a slit up the middle of one halfway. Cut down the middle of the other halfway.

Put the two circles together. Decorate and hang.

All of the Christmas decorations you have now made were easy and didn't take too long. You probably didn't need much help either.

The next group of decorations should be projects that you do with someone older than you. Also, they require more time. Some of them must dry overnight. You will also need some special supplies.

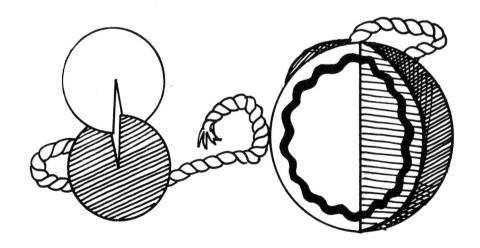

Clay Decorations

Before you begin read through the instructions. Get all of the materials you need. Be sure to take your time and have a lot of fun working on these.

You will need—

    2 Cups of Baking Soda

    1 Cup of Cornstarch

    Paint or Magic Markers

    Shellac (if you want)

    Metal Cookie Cutters

    Waxpaper and a Rolling Pin

    A Pan

Have Mom or someone older do the following—

Put the baking soda and cornstarch in a pan. Stir in 1¼ cups of cold water. Stir until smooth. Then bring to a boil over medium heat. Keep stirring. Cook for one minute longer. It should look like moist mashed potatoes. (Try not to overcook as this will make your clay crumble.)

Remove the pan from the stove. Put the clay on a plate to cool. Cover with a damp towel.

When the clay is cool enough to hold, have Mom knead it a little for you. Then put the clay in a plastic bag. Use only as you need it.

Lay wax paper on your work area. Take a small ball and place on the wax paper. Using a rolling pin, roll the clay out until it is about ¼ inch thick.

Take your cookie cutters and cut out the shapes you want. You will need a hole to put the yarn through to hang your decorations. Put the hole in these by using a toothpick or a nail.

Let your decorations dry overnight. When they are completely hard they are ready to be decorated. This is the fun part. Decorate them any way you want. You can shellac them once your paint is dry. Then they are ready to hang.

These decorations are so much fun to make that you could even make a box of them to give to Grandpa and Grandma for a very special before Christmas present.

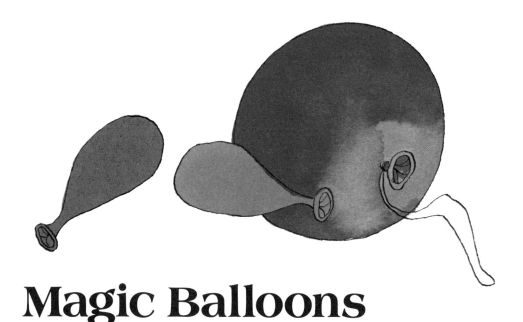

Magic Balloons

Again, read your instructions first. Get your supplies. Have fun!

You will need—

      Small Round Balloons

      Tissue Paper or Cloth (cut these into small strips)

      String or Yarn

      Newspaper (to keep the floor from getting wet)

      1 Cup Starch

Have Mom, or someone older, help with this—

Blow up your balloons first. Then tie a string around the top of each balloon. Tie it long enough to use to hang your decorations with when they are dry.

Now, you will need a place you can hang your balloons up on overnight to dry. Put newspaper under this area. The balloons will drip.

Put 1 cup of starch and 3 cups of cold water in a pan on the stove on low. Stir with a wooden spoon until the mixture is "sticky." Remove from the stove. Put the pan on a work area that is covered by newspaper.

Put a balloon in the mixture. Using your fingers, rub all over the balloon. Now take your tissue paper or cloth and put it in the pan.

Smooth each strip onto your balloon. Overlap the pieces. Wrap around several times. Hang up to dry.

In the morning when the tissue paper is hard, take a pin or needle and stick in the balloon. They are now ready to decorate and hang on your tree.

A DECORATION TO GIVE

Christmas is a happy time of year, and it is also a time of giving. Here's a decoration you can make and give to someone special. Be sure to give it early in December so that it can be used through the holiday. It's a Christmas Card Stocking!

You will need—

        felt

        thread

        scissors

        decorations (anything that you can find)

Make your stocking about 36 inches long. Sew pockets on to hold Christmas cards. Leave only the top of each pocket open. Glue on other decorations. They can be made from felt, sequins, glitter or other scraps from Mother's sewing box.

These are fun to make, and don't take long. Make one for Mother, Grandma and how 'bout one for the lady across the street?

Merry Christmas!

how to have fun

BAKING COOKIES AND CAKES
BUILDING SAILBOATS
KNITTING
WITH MACRAME
MAKING BIRDHOUSES AND FEEDERS
MAKING BREAKFAST
MAKING CHRISTMAS DECORATIONS
MAKING KITES
MAKING MOBILES
MAKING PAPER AIRPLANES
MAKING PUPPETS
WITH NEEDLEPOINT
SEWING
WEAVING
WITH AN INDOOR GARDEN

creative
craft
books

ESEA TITLE II 74